598.2

Series Editor: Lionel Bender

Published by Country Life Books,
an imprint of Newnes Books, a
Division of The Hamlyn Publishing Group Limited
84–88 The Centre, Feltham, Middlesex, England
and distributed for them by
The Hamlyn Publishing Group
Limited, Rushden, Northants, England
© Newnes Books, a Division of The Hamlyn Publishing
Group Limited 1985

ISBN 0 600 35771 6

Printed in Italy.

THE
COUNTRY LIFE POCKET GUIDE
TO
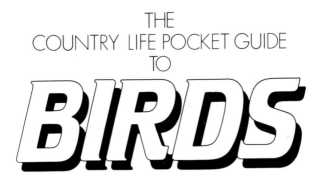

BIRDS

John Stidworthy

COUNTRY LIFE
BOOKS

Contents

Introduction

This book is intended as a guide to the birds of Britain and north-west Europe. It is not a comprehensive reference book for every kind of bird that lives in the area. Rather, it is an identification guide to the species that are likely to come to the attention of newcomers to birdwatching, interested weekend walkers and others with an interest in birds but without specialized knowledge.

In this volume will be found the birds that are to be noticed as you go through the countryside. Birds that are common in gardens, towns or countrywide. Birds that are common in particular habitats, such as the coast. There are also birds that are less common but are spectacular or have features of particular interest. On the other hand, groups that may be difficult for the relative novice to see or identify easily, such as some of the warblers and waders, are not dealt with exhaustively. In these cases, just a few of the more readily identified species are shown as examples.

The great majority of birds in this book can be seen regularly in Britain. A few are normally confined to the Continent. Where this is the case, it is clearly stated. All the species illustrated are recorded as having occurred in Britain at some time.

Occasionally there are colour differences between British examples of a bird and those on the Continent, as, for example, in the yellow wagtail. Where this occurs, both types are described, with differences noted. Where only one illustration is shown, this may be assumed to be the type found in Britain.

The birds are arranged in the book according to family groupings, so related – which often means similar-looking – birds are found on the same page or adjacent pages. For these groupings, you will find a brief description of their characteristics, followed by descriptions of the individual species.

For each species there is a colour illustration and a description of its appearance, together with notes on any characteristic postures or behaviour that may help indentification, Peculiarities of flight, or appearance in flight, may also be relevant, and these are noted and sometimes illustrated. Songs and sounds are also mentioned for some species, but sounds represented in print are notoriously subjective, and anyone with an interest in bird song would do well to purchase recordings to hear examples of bird voices.

Other details given for each kind of bird include the habitat in which you would expect to see them. Most birds have a preference for a particular type of countryside, but of course they can fly and sometimes turn up in unusual situations. The distribution of the bird, that is the geographical area it inhabits, is also given. In particular, any peculiarities in distribution in Britain are mentioned. Some birds are found countrywide, some are confined to a limited area. If no particular mention is made of distribution, it can be assumed to include suitable habitats throughout Britain.

Many of the birds described are residents, present in Britain all the year round. Others are migratory, coming from the south to make use of the long summer days, with their plentiful insect life, to nest and rear their young. In autumn, as the food supplies dwindle, the birds migrate south again, some travelling as far as southern Africa. There are also our winter visitors. These nest in the Arctic, northern Europe or eastern Europe, and escape the rigours of winter in these regions by moving south and west. Even among resident species there may be seasonal movements, and additional birds from the Continent may fly in for part of the year. Migratory movements are noted in the species descriptions.

A note on feeding habits will usually be found, either in the species description or that of the family. Nesting habits, and eggs, are not generally listed, but some are mentioned if they are of particular interest.

Britain has a wide range of habitats in a relatively small island, and this is good news for birdwatchers, who can find a similarly wide variety of birds. It is also a changing variety. There are the seasonal changes as migrants come and go. The birds that congregate in our gardens in winter may disperse back to the woods to nest in summer. There are long-term changes in a particular place as habitats alter. For example, a young plantation grows into a mature wood and as it does so the birds that live there change. This sort of change may be seen on a small scale in some gardens.

Some of the changes to our bird populations are man-made. In the past, new kinds of bird have been introduced to Britain. The little owl and the red-legged partridge are relative newcomers. Birds have also been wiped out, either by hunting or by causing changes in habitat. This happened to the great bustard and the sea eagle, both of which are now the subjects of re-introduction schemes. Some birds return of their own accord if the right conditions are re-established, as have avocets and ospreys. But if the full variety of birds is to be maintained in Britain it is necessary to keep the full variety of habitats, making sure that they are sufficiently undisturbed for the birds to flourish.

Divers

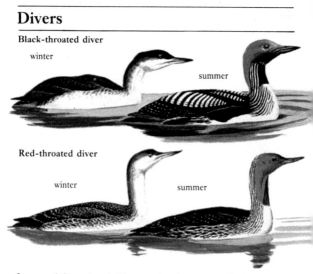

Black-throated diver

winter

summer

Red-throated diver

winter

summer

In general divers have bold patterns but these are not always easy to see at a distance. In summer the dull red throat patch, stripes on the back of the neck, and lack of wing pattern distinguish the swimming red-throated diver from the black-throated. The latter has a black throat patch, stripes on the side of the neck and on the wings. In winter the throat patches disappear, but the red-throated diver, being thinner and lighter in colour, is more obviously spotted.

Divers, as their name suggests, are specialized swimming birds. They have large webbed feet on legs that are set right at the rear of the body. Awkward on land, they go there only to nest. They swim low in the water, and may jump up and forward to begin a dive for food or may just slip gently underwater. They feed on fish and some crustaceans. In flight divers trail their legs and droop their necks, and their long narrow wings beat fast.

The red-throated diver *Gavia stellata* is 55cm long. In summer it may be seen on pools and lakes on moorland in Scotland, northern Ireland and northern Europe. In winter it is also offshore. Characteristically the red-throated diver swims with its bill tilted upward. The call is a fast quacking. Two eggs are laid in a nest right at the water's edge.

The black-throated diver *G. arctica* is a little larger and stouter than the red-throated, but less common. In summer it is found on large lakes in moorlands and forests, and in winter mainly offshore. In Britain it breeds only in Scotland.

Grebes

summer

winter

Great crested grebes of both sexes in summer have crests and neck frills. In winter the crests are reduced and the neck frills disappear, giving the birds a much whiter look.

The little grebe in summer has a chestnut throat and a light patch at the bill base. Its winter plumage is drabber.

winter

summer

Grebes are smaller than divers but are also adapted for swimming and diving. They have short legs set well back, but have lobed rather than webbed toes. The feet are trailed and the head is carried low in flight. Both sexes help build the nest, a mound of floating vegetation.

The great crested grebe *Podiceps cristatus* is 47cm long and the largest European grebe, with in summer the double-horned dark crest that gives it its name and a brown frill round the neck. It is found on lakes, reservoirs and flooded gravel pits with large areas of open water. Here it dives for small fishes, insects, tadpoles and crustaceans. In winter some birds move to coasts.

In spring the great crested grebe takes part in elaborate courtship rituals. The pair 'dance' upright face-to-face in the water or exchange presents of waterweed, as well as take part in fast chases. After hatching, the striped chicks may hitch a lift on a parent's back as it swims along.

The little grebe or dabchick *P. ruficollis* is only 25cm long, and has a rather round, tail-less body. It is found on lakes, ponds, canals and slow rivers. It likes areas with plenty of reeds and other cover.

Gannet and Manx shearwater

The Manx shearwater is dark above and white below. The wingbeat is fast, interspersed with long glides.

The gannet is the largest seabird of north European waters. It has very long wings with conspicuous black tips, and a pointed head and tail.

The gannet *Sula bassana* reaches 90cm in length. White, with black-tipped wings, it is a plunge diver, flying or soaring up to 40m above the water before partly folding its wings, diving and plunging underwater to capture a fish. Sometimes flocks of gannets gather above shoaling fish. After feeding gannets may rest on the sea, but spend most of the time in the air, where the size, shape and the brilliant white of their plumage are distinctive. They may fish far from their breeding grounds.

Gannets breed at a limited number of sites, mostly offshore islands whose steep cliffs and rocks are inaccessible except to birds. Outside the breeding season the birds disperse. A single egg is laid and incubated under the large webbed feet. On each foot all four toes are joined in the web.

The Manx shearwater *Puffinus puffinus* lays its single egg in a burrow, often in dense colonies with others of its kind. It breeds on a small number of islands off Ireland and western Britain. Movement to and from the colonies is at night. Only 35cm long, the shearwater spends most of its life at sea and eats small fish and squid.

Shag and Cormorant

The **shag** has a small crest on its head during the breeding season.

non-breeding

breeding

The **cormorant** is larger than the shag and has a white chin patch. Continental cormorants, but not usually those of Britain and Norway, have white over much of the head. In the breeding season there is a white patch on the thigh.

Continental form

Atlantic form (breeding)

Atlantic form (non-breeding)

These are large dark-coloured birds with a long bill, hooked at the tip, and large feet with four toes in the web. They swim very low in the water and are expert divers. They may be seen perched on rocks or posts with their wings stretched out to dry. In flight they have rather stiff wingbeats, a broad tail, and the head is carried well up.

The shag *Phalacrocorax aristotelis* is only 75cm long. It rarely comes inland, but goes farther out to sea than the cormorant, fishing in deeper water and catching fewer bottom-living fish.

The cormorant *P. carbo* is 90cm long. In western Europe it is mainly a coastal bird, found especially along sheltered rocky coasts, but also on rivers and reservoirs. Many bottom-living fish are included in its diet.

Both birds make a nest of sticks or seaweed on rock shelves. On the Continent cormorants may nest in trees.

Heron, Bittern and Stork

The heron trails its long legs in flight but folds its neck so the head is close to the body. The wings are huge and rounded, the wingbeat slow and majestic.

The heron's mainly grey and white plumage has black markings on the front of the neck and on the edge of each wing. The crest and the stripe behind the eye are also black.

The bittern is well camouflaged, but in spring the male's foghorn-like 'boom' may be heard more than a kilometre away.

Herons are long-legged wading birds that feed on small animals in all kinds of shallow water. They catch their prey using the long dagger-shaped beak like a pair of forceps. The feet have four long toes which spread the weight when on soft mud.

The grey heron *Ardea cinerea* is 90cm long. It is grey on its back and wings; the underside, neck and head are white. At the back of the head is a drooping crest.

The white stork is unmistakable, with its white plumage and black wing-feathers and large red bill and red legs.

White storks are mostly silent, but at the nest a bill-clattering display is heard.

Stork wingbeats are slow, and the birds often soar.

nest on rooftop

Herons may be seen either stalking prey or waiting motionless for it. At rest they often stand with head sunk on to shoulders, the long neck folded. They nest in colonies, usually building their stick nest in trees.

The bittern *Botaurus stellaris* is 75cm long. Streaked brown and spending much of its time in dense reed-beds, it is not easy to spot. Its stronghold in Britain is East Anglia, but it does occur elsewhere.

Storks are very large birds with long legs and very large, pointed beaks. Only two species are found in Europe, both as summer visitors, and neither is found regularly in Britain. On the wing, storks fly slowly with both legs and neck extended. The tips of the huge wings have separated feathers.

The white stork *Ciconia ciconia* is 100cm long. It nests in Denmark, the Low Countries and from Germany eastward. It is nearly always associated with humans, and nests on buildings, poles and other man-made structures as well as in trees. In spite of this, over the years storks have declined in number and in many parts of their range disappeared completely. It is doubtful if the white stork ever nested regularly in Britain. However, individuals are sometimes seen in the south-east during their migration.

The white stork forages in marshes, wet meadows and grassland, catching and eating a variety of animals that ranges from beetles and grasshoppers to rats and snakes.

Swans

Swans are often seen in family groups. Here a young cygnet keeps close to its mother, with father also in attendance.

Swans use their long necks to gather water vegetation.

The mute swan builds a large nest. It may be fiercely protective of its nest or young.

Swans are huge, long-necked birds of lakes, rivers and sheltered seashores. They include some of the heaviest flying birds. All the European species have white plumage as adults, but their beaks have distinctive colours. They feed on waterweeds, dipping their head and neck into the water to gather them from the bottom.

The mute swan *Cygnus olor* is up to 150cm long. The bill is pinkish-orange with a black base. Both sexes have a black knob above the base of the bill, larger in the male. The young birds, cygnets, have greyish-brown plumage.

This species of swan swims with its neck in a graceful curve, bill pointed downward, and often with its wing-

Whooper swans are as large, but have straight necks and straight bills with a large area of yellow. Bewick's swans are smaller and have more black on the bill.

Bewick's swan

Mute swan

Whooper swan

The mute swan has an orange bill with a knob at the base.

feathers raised above its back. It signals aggression to other swans by arching its wings.

Native to Britain, Germany, the Low Countries and the southern Baltic, the mute swan has been introduced to many places as an ornamental bird. It nests close to water, building a huge mound of weeds in which five to seven eggs are laid. The swans breed in spring and incubation takes five weeks. The young can soon swim and grow rapidly, but do not fly for four months. It is several years before they have complete adult plumage.

Despite its name, the mute swan makes grunts, hisses and gurgles. In flight, wingbeats make a loud rhythmic singing sound. A flock often flies in line or V-formation, each bird with its head and neck outstretched.

The whooper swan *C. cygnus* is as large as the mute swan but has a yellow and black bill with no knob at the base. It keeps its neck straight when swimming and its wingbeats are quiet. Mainly a winter visitor, this species is less common than the mute swan.

Bewick's swan *C. columbianus* is an uncommon winter visitor. No more than 120cm long, it is the smallest of the European swans. It resembles the whooper swan, but has a smaller beak and rounder head. Bewick's and the whooper swan both make trumpeting calls.

17

Geese

The **greylag goose** has a very pale grey front to its wings that may show up in flight. Wingbeats are strong and stately but the bird tends to roll and swoop in the air before landing.

The **greylag goose** is solid-looking with a large head and neck and thick bill. The pale grey body has a white patch beneath the tail. The feet are pink and the bill orange.

Geese are large, plump waterfowl with long necks and webbed feet. The legs are placed well forward under the body and geese walk confidently. They find most of their food by grazing on the land, cropping grass and picking up grain with their broad, round-ended beaks. Sexes look alike.

The greylag goose *Anser anser* is up to 89cm long. It is mainly grey in colour but has white below the tail, and has pink legs and feet. It has a thick neck and a noticeably large strong orange bill.

This is the ancestor of the farm goose and shares its honking call and habit of hissing at intruders. Wild greylags, however, are normally very wary birds.

The greylag goose breeds in coastal areas of Scandinavia, in Denmark, Germany and Britain. The main British breeding grounds are in Scotland, particularly the Outer Hebrides, but greylags may be found breeding elsewhere in Britain, some at least as the result of deliberate introduction.

Canada geese have a strong, fast flight. They often fly in large groups in V-formation but also in irregular flocks.

The Canada goose is unmistakable with its brown back, light underside, and black head and neck with strongly contrasting white chin-patch.

The brent goose is small and dark. The neck is short and the bill small. Only a small whitish patch interrupts the black of head and neck.

Greylags breed in colonies, often choosing moorland areas with pools. In winter they move to salt- or freshwater marshes and often feed on agricultural land. Flocks often fly in V-formation.

The brent goose *Branta bernicla* is, at 60cm long, scarcely larger than a mallard duck. It breeds in the high Arctic, but regularly comes to the coasts of western Europe to winter. In Britain it is most likely to be seen on mudflats and estuaries on the east or south coasts. It flies in irregular flocks rather than in V-formation.

The Canada goose *B. canadensis* is a large goose up to 100cm long. Brown-bodied, but with a distinctive white chin-patch on the black head and neck, this goose originated in Canada but introductions and escapes have allowed it to establish itself in Britain and Sweden. Especially in southern England it is now quite common on lakes and nearby grassland.

Ducks 1

The mallard is the most familiar duck. Drake mallards have a yellow bill and black curved feathers just above the tail.

The shoveler has a rather flat head and a long flat bill.

Shovelers of both sexes have a pale blue forewing and a green wing-patch behind.

Shoveler

Ducks are small waterfowl with short necks, short legs and webbed feet. In most European species the male or drake differs in colour from the female and has brighter plumage, except during the late summer when the male moults to 'eclipse' plumage like that of the female. There are two main groups of duck, the diving ducks and the dabbling ducks. The latter feed from the surface.

The mallard *Anas platyrhynchos*, at 58cm in length, is one of the largest ducks. It is also the most widespread.

The wild male mallard has a green head, white neck band and chestnut breast. The female is speckled brown, as are juveniles. Both sexes have on the back of the wings a purplish-blue patch with a strip of white in front and behind.

Mallards swim high in the water. They feed on a large

Teals are small and short-necked. A green and black wing-patch shows in flight.

male

Teal

female

male

female

Wigeon

The wigeon is a compact-looking duck with a comparatively short beak. The head colouring of the male is distinctive.

variety of food ranging from waterweed to fish.

The shoveler *A. clypeata* is superficially like a mallard, the female speckled brown and the drake with a green head, although it has a white chest and chestnut belly. But the shoveler is a smaller bird, only about 50cm long, and sits lower in the water with a rather short-necked look. The bill is big and broad.

The teal *A. crecca* is only 35cm long, the smallest of the European ducks, with a rather chubby look. The drake's chestnut head with green eye-stripe is distinctive at close quarters, but at a distance it may just look dark compared to a grey body. The female is coloured like a female mallard.

Although common, the teal prefers pools and marshes surrounded with vegetation. It is a fast and agile flier.

The wigeon *A. penelope* is 46cm long. The drake has a chestnut head with a cream forehead, a pinkish breast and a grey body. The beak is rather small. The wings are very long and pointed.

The wigeon breeds in Denmark, Scandinavia and northern Britain by inland waters. In winter it may be on estuaries. It gathers in large flocks and spends much time grazing on land.

These four species of duck each build their nests in hollows in the ground, usually near to water.

Ducks 2

female male

Tufted duck are very common. The tuft and colouring make males easy to recognize. Tufted duck are usually active, jumping upward as they start a dive.

female

The eider can be distinguished by its large size and straight forehead. It dives from the surface to eat mussels, shellfish and crustaceans.

male

The tufted duck *Aythya fuligula* is one of the diving ducks. They dive below the surface to search for food, propelling themselves with their webbed feet which are set well back. Diving ducks patter across the surface when taking off to fly, unlike the almost vertical take-off of most dabbling ducks.

Tufted ducks grow to 43cm long. The drake appears black except for the contrasting white side and belly. He has a drooping tuft of feathers at the back of the head, and yellow eyes. The female is brown rather than black, with just the hint of a tuft, and no white patch.

In the breeding season the tufted duck is found on lakes and pools where there is cover around the banks. It is commonly seen in parks. In winter it is found, sometimes in large aggregations, on larger bodies of fresh water such as reservoirs.

The eider *Somateria mollissima* is a sea duck, seen swimming offshore in groups. It is large, 58cm long, and has an unusual profile, the forehead being in line with the strong beak. The black belly and white back of the

The shelduck nests in a burrow, usually an old rabbit burrow in sand dunes, or in thick cover.

Shelduck in flight can be identified by the bold pattern and goose-like shape. The wingbeats are slower than those of most ducks.

female

male

juvenile male

Shelduck sexes are similar, but the male has a red knob at the base of the beak. The female has no knob, but has a white line around the base of the beak.

male are distinctive. There is also a black eye-stripe and lime-green nape. The female is brown.

This species lives and breeds around the coasts of northern Europe, including northern Britain. Some individuals may be seen further south. It builds its nests among rocks or vegetation near the water's edge.

The shelduck *Tadorna tadorna* is 60cm long. This large duck has a goose-like shape and a mainly black and white plumage. A chestnut band extends round the chest and neck. The legs are pink. The beak is red, and has a red knob at the base in the male.

Shelducks are mostly seen on coasts, sometimes inland. Typically they feed in large groups on estuaries and mudflats. In late summer, they congregate in a few areas in very large numbers for the moult. At this time the young of the year may be left behind in a 'creche' with a few adults in charge.

Game birds 1

male

female

Pheasants in flight have long, wide-spread tails and rather short rounded wings. They usually fly low, with rapid wingbeats followed by glides.

female

male

The hen pheasant incubates the eggs in a nest on the ground and tends the young. Her mottled brown plumage gives good camouflage. The male pheasant takes no part in the rearing of the young, and has bright plumage for display.

Game birds are chicken-like species with heavy bodies. They can fly, but spend most of their time on the ground looking for the seeds and insects which make up their diet. They can run well and if disturbed will often run for cover first rather than flying away.

Female game birds are mainly dull, camouflaged colours. In some species the males are more brightly coloured and are larger.

The pheasant *Phasianus colchicus* is common throughout much of Europe, except northern Scandinavia. Not originally native, it has been introduced for sport.

The male pheasant in 84cm long, including the 45cm-long tail. The female is 58cm, 23cm of which is tail.

They are birds of woods and thick cover, but often emerge into fields to forage for food. They do not take to flight very readily, but when they do so have a very noisy, almost vertical, take-off. They fly strongly for

The red-legged partridge is more strikingly marked than the common partridge. The red bill, legs, and white cheeks surrounded by black, are characteristic.

The partridge is clad in subdued colours in both sexes, but at close quarters the adults can be seen to have an attractive pattern.

juvenile

female

male

short distances, hard flapping alternating with long glides.

The partridge *Perdix perdix* is a round-bodied, short-tailed bird about 30cm long. It often appears a dull brown, but closer inspection reveals a chestnut face and throat with a grey breast, and a dark patch on the belly that is more pronounced in males.

This game bird is found on farmland and heaths. Its nest is a scrape among crops or under bushes. It runs fast with its head up. If it takes off, the short wings whirr, interspersed with glides, as it travels over the ground.

The partridge has declined in Britain, possibly due to the effects of pesticides on the insects which are important as food for the young.

The red-legged partridge *Alectoris rufa* is 34cm long. Originally an inhabitant of dry country in Spain and southern France, it has been introduced into Britain, where it breeds particularly in the south and east.

Game birds 2

The red grouse male is a darker colour and slightly larger than the female. Both are well camouflaged in their moorland home and may not be noticed until they are flushed from the heather. The legs are white with feathered toes.

male, summer

male, summer

female, summer

The ptarmigan is all white in winter plumage, except for black tail feathers. Ptarmigan change plumage three times a year.

female, autumn

male, winter

The red grouse *Lagopus lagopus* is up to 40cm long. It is rather heavily built, with dark reddish-brown barred plumage, the hens a little smaller and paler than the cocks. The red grouse is found only in Britain and Ireland, but it belongs to the same species as the willow grouse found in Scandinavia, which has a varying amount of white in its plumages throughout the year.

The grouse lives on moorland and so in Britain is found only in the north and west. It is vegetarian, feeding largely on various parts of the heather plant, along with some other buds and berries. The grouse remains on the moors throughout the year. The flight is fast, keeping low and gliding between rapid bursts.

The ptarmigan *L. mutus* is 35cm long. It lives on mountain tops above the tree line. It is found in the northernmost parts of Europe, including the Scottish mountains. In winter it is almost completely white. In summer the wings remain white but the body is dark brown-grey above. At all seasons it is difficult to see on the ground and is reluctant to fly.

Birds of prey 1

The sparrowhawk in flight shows broad rounded wings, a fairly long tail and barred underparts. It flies fast.

male

Hen harrier female

male

female

The male sparrowhawk is much redder below than the female.

The male hen harrier is grey, rather than brown like the female, and is differently patterned on chest and underparts. In both sexes there is a white patch on the rump.

female

male

Birds of prey are flesh-eating birds that hunt in daylight. They have strong, sharp, curved talons to seize and kill their prey, and powerful hooked bills to tear at their food. Their keen eyes are placed facing forward so they are able to judge distances when hunting on the wing. In many species the female is larger than the male and the two sexes may hunt a different range of food. Most nest singly in remote places.

The sparrowhawk *Accipiter nisus* is up to 38cm long. It is common throughout Europe, mainly in areas of woodland and among copses and hedgerows. It hunts sparrows and other small birds, flying low and fast along woodland edges and taking them by surprise.

The hen harrier *Circus cyaneus* is up to 50cm long. It is found over most of Europe. In Britain it breeds in Scotland, northern England and Wales on moorland. In winter it may be seen in lowland heaths and dunes.

The hunting flight is buoyant but low, a few flaps of the wing preceding a glide. It feeds on small ground-living animals.

Birds of prey 2

The male kestrel has a richer plumage than the female. The blue-grey head and tail are distinctive.

male

male

female

The kestrel is expert at hovering several metres up. As it glides or flies to a new hovering position it shows its long tail and narrow pointed wings.

The kestrel *Falco tinnunculus* is up to 34cm long. Both sexes are red-brown on back and wings, the female barred, the male spotted. Both sexes have a black band at the end of the tail.

Colours are not always easy to see on the wing, but the shape and way of flying are characteristic. The kestrel has long, pointed wings and a long tail. It is most often seen hovering in one spot while it surveys the ground below for prey. As it does this the tail is fanned and the wings vibrate fast, the forward flight just counteracting the effects of the wind.

Common throughout Europe, including the whole of Britain, the kestrel may be seen in almost any kind of open country. It can even be seen in cities. It makes a habit of hovering over motorway verges, looking for the voles, mice and beetles which make up its diet.

The buzzard *Buteo buteo* is up to 56cm long. It is an accomplished soarer and can ride air currents for hours

The buzzard in flight has very broad wings and the head looks short.

Buzzards vary considerably in colour. British birds are usually fairly dark, with brown rather than whitish chests as here.

adult

The golden eagle has long powerful wings. The wingtips are usually spread and splayed up.

The golden eagle has a powerful bill and huge talons. The legs are 'trousered' in feathers.

on outstretched wings, lazily sweeping to-and-fro. The wings are big and broad, with separated feathers at the tips. It looks short-necked in flight and the tail is broad.

Buzzards are often seen perched on posts and telegraph poles searching the ground for prey.

They are found throughout much of Europe, but leave the northernmost parts in winter. In Britain the buzzard lives largely in the north and west. It feeds on carrion and animals up to the size of rabbits.

The golden eagle *Aquila chrysaetos* is up to 88cm long. A huge, powerful bird, it is the commonest of Europe's eagles and lives especially in mountain areas. In Britain it lives mainly in the Scottish Highlands but in recent years a few have returned to northern England.

Adults are mainly brown, with 'golden' feathers on the back of the neck. Youngsters have white in the plumage. Golden eagles soar well, but will often glide low along a mountain ridge looking for prey.

Rail, Moorhen and Coot

Coot flight looks weak, with legs trailing, but individuals fly well enough for some continental birds to migrate to Britain for the winter.

Adult coots are unmistakable, with a white front to the head and a black body. The feet have huge lobed toes.

Young coots lack the contrasting black and white of their parents.

chick

Coots are social birds and can often be seen displaying or fighting.

Rails and their allies are medium-sized birds with short necks and chunky compact bodies. The legs are quite long and the toes large. Most live in or around water or swamps.

The coot *Fulica atra* is 38cm long. In the water it looks black except for the beak and the white shield above. The legs and feet are distinctive, with large lobed toes used in swimming. Common throughout western Europe except for Scandinavia, the coot is found throughout the British Isles on lakes, reservoirs and large park ponds. The coot dives for its food and eats water plants as well as insects and small fish. It makes an upward jump before submerging.

In addition to being a good swimmer and diver the coot can walk and run well, although its feet are very large. It makes a nest in the form of a platform of reeds moored in shallow water.

The coot has a running take-off and flies rather weakly, low across the water with legs trailing. Coots sometimes

The adult moorhen has a red front to the head and yellow-green legs. The white feathers are conspicuous against the dark plumage. In juveniles the plumage is much browner and the beak and front of the head lack the distinctive coloration.

Moorhens make short, weak-looking flights although they tend to move through the air quite fast.

chick

The water rail is secretive, but when it is seen the long red bill is a distinctive feature.

juvenile

chick

congregate in large numbers but are rather quarrelsome.

The moorhen *Gallinula chloropus* is smaller than the coot, only 33cm long and less bulky, and has long thin toes with no lobes. The base of the bill and the frontal shield are red. A white line shows on the flanks, and below the tail is a white patch which is conspicuous because the moorhen constantly flicks its tail.

Moorhens are found in all kinds of freshwater habitats, usually where there is vegetation round the banks.

The water rail *Rallus aquaticus* is about 28cm long. It is not easy to see as it spends much time in thick cover in swamps and marshes. If it does emerge, the long red bill is a good recognition feature.

The rail is heard more often than seen, as it makes loud squeals, grunts and sharp calls.

Except for northern Scandinavia the water rail occurs in most parts of western Europe where there is suitable habitat. In Britain it is commoner in winter, when migrants add to the resident population.

Lapwing, Curlew and Redshank

In flight, lapwings appear dark above but show white patches below on the inner wings and breast.

Lapwings may be well camouflaged in a field, although once spotted they are easy to recognize by their crests and dark and light colouring.

juvenile

Birds such as these are waders which, as the name suggests, are species associated with the water's edge, in which they may wade but do not swim. They are medium to small in size, have relatively long legs and, in many cases, long bills.

The lapwing *Vanellus vanellus* is 30cm long. It is easy to recognize by the crest which sticks up from the back of the head. At a distance it appears black above, white below. Close to, the dark parts are dark glossy green.

Lapwings are seen in fields, marshes and moors, usually in flocks. When feeding they walk or run a few paces, then tip forward to pick up an insect or worm.

In flight the lapwing shows broad rounded wings, which it uses with slow wingbeats. Its flight may not be very direct. At times, especially in the breeding season, it can be seen performing aerobatics, twisting and sideslipping in the air. Seasonal movements of lapwings take place, many moving from fields to estuaries and

Curlew flight is strong. The long bill and white rump-patch may show.

The curlew has a long down-curved bill. It is a rather uniform speckled colour, and is bigger than other waders.

summer

The redshank's bright legs are a good identifying feature. It is also noisy, making yelping calls.

The redshank in flight shows a white rump and a broad white band at the back of each wing.

adjacent coasts in winter. Migrants from the Continent also arrive in Britain in winter. The call of the lapwing, 'pee-wit', gives it its alternative English name.

The curlew *Numenius arquata* is 56cm long, and the biggest of the waders. It has a whistling 'cur-lew' call.

In summer most curlews nest on moorland, but they are also found in other damp habitats throughout Britain except the south-east. In winter they are most likely to be seen on estuaries and mudflats, but also occur on wet meadows. The bill is used to probe in mud for the small invertebrates that make up much of the diet.

The redshank *Tringa totanus* is 28cm long. Mainly speckled brown in appearance, the base of the bill is red and the long orange-red legs give the bird its name.

Common in suitable locations throughout the British Isles, the redshank is often seen feeding on estuaries and muddy shores, singly or in flocks. It breeds on salt-marshes, wet meadows and moors.

Dunlin, Plovers and Turnstone

Dunlin fly in fast, low, cloud-like flocks. The birds have dark rumps.

Dunlin differ in winter and summer plumages, but the long down-curved bill is a constant recognition feature.

winter

summer

The **ringed plover** has bold markings but is difficult to see on the shore. At close range, the black markings on the head and the yellow legs and beak confirm its identity.

Ringed plovers fly fast and low, with fast wingbeats.

juvenile

The dunlin *Calidris alpina* is 18cm long. It is the most numerous of the small waders. Its plumage differs between winter and summer. The winter plumage is streaked grey, lighter below. Summer plumage is chestnut streaked with black above, with a conspicuous black patch on the belly. The beak is rather long and slightly down-curved.

This species breeds on boggy moorland. In Britain it breeds mainly in Scotland and northern England. Outside the breeding season it is found on estuaries and mudflats. During migration and in winter numbers are boosted by flocks from northern Europe.

Dunlin are often seen in big flocks, flying fast in unison, twisting and turning low over the shore. On the ground they look hunched-up as they probe for food.

The ringed plover *Charadrius hiaticula* is 19cm long. Grey-brown above and white below, it has a small bill. It lives and nests along the seashore, where adults, eggs

winter   summer

The **turnstone** lives up to its
name, picking over the debris on
the shore. The summer plumage
of black, white and chestnut is
particularly distinctive.

Often flying in huge packs of V-
formations, golden plovers are
extremely agile in the air. Their
pointed, angled wings in flight
are distinctive.

The **golden plover** has a
spangling of gold and black on its
back at all seasons, but brightest
in summer, when it also sports
dark underparts.

summer   winter

and young are difficult for enemies to see. Unfortunately
in this situation they are very vulnerable to human
disturbance and their numbers have declined.

The turnstone *Arenaria interpres* is 23cm long and
stockily built. Black-brown and white in winter, with
added bright chestnut on the back in summer, the
turnstone is nevertheless inconspicuous. It uses its short
but powerful bill to turn over stones and seaweed as it
searches for food. It frequents rocky and stony shores
and is rarely seen in big flocks. Breeding birds go to nest
in the Arctic. Most turnstones seen in Britain are winter
visitors.

The golden plover *Pluvialis apricaria* is about 28cm
long. It has a gold and black back. In summer there are
black markings on the throat and breast. In winter it is
whitish below. The golden plover breeds on moorland
in northern and western Britain. Out of the breeding
season it may be seen on farmland and mudflats.

Oystercatcher and Avocet

The oystercatcher is a large, short-necked, black and white wader with a long and powerful orange-red bill.

juvenile

chick

The avocet is a slender black and white wader with long neck and legs, and a long thin upturned bill.

The oystercatcher *Haematopus ostralegus* is a large wader 43cm long. It is found on all coasts and also breeds by water and on moorland in northern Britain. Its call of 'deep, deep' draws attention. The flight is strong and straight with shallow wingbeats, and when in the air a white band along each wing is conspicuous.

The avocet *Recurvirostra avosetta* is 43cm long. It is fairly common in suitable habitats from southern Sweden southward into Europe, but at one time was extinct in Britain. It has returned as a breeding bird to East Anglia in the last 40 years or so.

Arctic skua

The Arctic skua occurs in two colour phases. A higher proportion of dark birds are seen in the south of the breeding range, as at the northern tip of Britain.

dark phase

light phase

Immature Arctic skuas are speckled brown. They have long, pointed wings but lack the two long tail feathers characteristic of adults.

Swimming buoyantly with tails raised, Arctic skuas spend much time on the sea.

juvenile

Skuas are seabirds akin to gulls with dark plumage and tails with elongated central feathers. They are 'pirates', often chasing and harassing gulls and terns until these disgorge their last meal. As well as feeding on these remains they will take eggs and chicks of other species.

The Arctic skua *Stercorarius parasiticus* is about 46cm long. The upper body and top of the head are always dark brown. The underside may be dark brown or light, and intermediates occur. In mature birds two central tail feathers are elongated.

This, the most common skua, breeds in Scandinavia and the extreme north of Scotland, Orkney and Shetland, nesting on moorland away from the sea. It may be seen off most British coasts in autumn as it travels to the southern oceans for the winter.

The Arctic skua is a graceful flier on its long, pointed wings and is acrobatic in pursuit of other birds such as terns.

Gulls

The herring gull has a grey back and wings. The eyes look fierce, the strong bill is yellow with a red spot, and the legs are flesh colour.

The juvenile herring gull is brown and changes to adult plumage over several years.

juvenile

Gulls are medium to large seabirds with webbed feet and strong beaks. Most have white plumage with grey or black backs. They fly and glide well on long pointed wings. Some species are found well inland. Many are opportunist feeders. As well as settling on water to catch fish they may raid garbage dumps, catch insects or follow the farm plough for worms.

The herring gull *Larus argentatus* is, at 56cm long, a large and powerful bird. It has silver-grey upperparts with a black tip to each wing. Most western European individuals have flesh-pink legs, but in Scandinavia the legs are yellow. Young birds are speckled brown, changing to adult plumage by about three years old.

This species is the commonest British gull, found on most coasts, and often foraging inland. It has a slow but strong flight, and glides well. It may be seen following ships for offal or gliding above cliffs. It has a loud 'keeow, keeow' call.

The great black-backed gull *L. marinus* is, at 69cm long, the largest gull likely to be seen in western Europe. It has a huge body, flesh-coloured legs and a yellow bill

The kittiwake is a neat-looking gull with a plain yellow bill and black feet. The eyes are dark. Juveniles have a black stripe down each wing.

adult

juvenile

The lesser black-backed gull is slender, and has a dark grey back and yellow legs.

The great black-backed gull's huge size, black back and pink legs help to identify it.

with a red spot. The back, and the top of the wings, are black. Either on the wing, in slow strong flight, or just standing, it looks a very powerful bird.

Most great black-backed gulls stay by the sea. In Britain they breed mainly on the western coasts, making their nests on cliff-tops.

The lesser black-backed gull *L. fuscus* is only 53cm long, much smaller than the great black-backed. It has yellow legs and looks more lightly built. British individuals are also a lighter colour on their backs than the larger species. The lesser black-backed gull is mainly a summer visitor, although some now overwinter. It breeds mostly in western and northern Britain.

The kittiwake *Rissa tridactyla* is 41cm long. It spends most of its time out at sea but nests in large colonies on steep sea cliffs, where birds may be heard giving their 'kit-ee-wake' cry. The feet are black, and the black wing-tips are unbroken by white spots.

Black-headed gull and Common tern

The **black-headed gull** has a dark brown head and red bill. In winter the dark head is lost, but a dark smudge behind the eye remains.

winter

summer

The **common tern** has a dark cap and black-tipped red bill. The long pointed wings, long forked tail and graceful flying earned terns the name 'sea-swallows'.

The black-headed gull *Larus ridibundus* is a small gull only 38cm long. The head is not black, but chocolate brown. The beak and the legs are red.

In flight the black-headed gull looks buoyant. It often glides. The wings are very pointed and the front edges are white.

Black-headed gulls are often seen inland. Many winter around cities. They scavenge refuse and forage on arable land. Breeding colonies are usually on moors or dunes.

Terns are similar to gulls but generally smaller. They are slim-bodied and have long, pointed wings and forked tails. They have a buoyant flight, often with head and pointed bill directed downward as they search for small fish. They may hover before plunging from the air after prey. The legs are rather short.

The common tern *Sterna hirundo* is 35cm long. A black cap extends over the top of the head and the beak is orange-red with a black tip. It can be seen round much of the coast of Britain in summer months, diving for small fish such as sand-eels.

Razorbill and Puffin

The razorbill is thickset with an upright stance on land. The neck is short and the bill large.

Razorbills swim high in the water.

Puffins are unmistakable with their large bright beaks and orange feet. They often hold a row of small fish in the beak when returning to the nest.

The auk family, to which these two species belong, are seabirds which dive for food, propelling themselves underwater with their wings. They come ashore to breed but spend most of their lives at sea. The wings are short and beat very fast in flight. The feet are set far back, the neck is short, and the birds have an upright stance.

The razorbill *Alca torda* is 41cm long. Black on its head and back, it has a white front. The bill which gives its name is large and deep. In winter, adults have a white cheek-patch like young birds. Razorbills are common but stay out at sea except when nesting.

The puffin *Fratercula arctica* is only 30cm long. It breeds around the west and north coasts of Britain in suitable localities – inaccessible islands and cliffs with grassy slopes in which it can burrow to make its nest.

41

Pigeons and Doves 1

Town pigeons come in a variety of colours, but many resemble their wild ancestor.

The rock dove has a white rump and two strong black bars on each wing.

Pigeons and doves are rather plump birds with small heads. They waddle as they walk. They fly fast and well. Most kinds live where there are trees for perching and nesting. Mainly plant-eating, some species may be pests of crops.

The rock dove *Columba livia* is 33cm long. The original habitat of this bird was cliffs with ledges and caves for nesting, and some wild populations still occur in isolated parts of northern and western Scotland. This species, however, is the ancestor of domestic pigeons. Pigeons 'gone wild' from domestic stock are found almost everywhere man is, particularly in cities which provide 'cliffs'. These feral pigeons far outnumber truly wild individuals.

The wild colour is greyish with bars on the wings, and a white rump. Feral pigeons can also be brown, black, white or a mixture of colours.

Intelligent and adaptable, the town pigeon finds much of its food from man's activities. Wild rock doves forage away from their cliffs for seeds, grain and other vegetable matter. The pigeon flies fast and straight. It may occur in large flocks.

Woodpigeons have plump pink breasts and obvious white neck-patches.

The stock dove has no white in the plumage, and lacks the strong wing-bars of the rock dove.

The woodpigeon has a noisy take-off. The white bands on the wings are conspicuous in flight.

The woodpigeon *C. palumbus* is 40cm long. It appears even larger as it has a large tubby body and comparatively small head. It has a pink breast and a vivid white patch on each side of the neck. There is also a white patch on the angle of the wings which shows as a white bar in flight.

Woodpigeons live in farmland with plenty of trees, as well as in woods, and are found increasingly in gardens and even cities. Outside the breeding season large flocks may be seen, and they can devastate crops.

This species roosts and nests in trees, laying two white eggs as do most pigeons. Woodpigeons, however, are unusual in that they mostly breed in late summer.

The stock dove *C. oenas* is 33cm long, about the same size as the rock dove. It is a rather uniform colour and has a grey rump, not white. The bars on the wing are much less developed than in the rock dove.

Stock doves are fairly common in woods and farmland, and may be seen feeding on open fields in winter. They do form small flocks but are most likely to be seen in pairs.

Collared and Turtle doves

The **collared dove** gives the impression of being a plain colour, but the dark collar is a good identifying feature.

The **turtle dove** is very small and has a reddish upperside patterned with black, with a striped patch on each side of the neck.

The collared dove *Streptopelia decaocto* is about 30cm long, and almost uniformly coloured. It is sandy brown with a pinker tinge to the breast. There is a black collar bordered with white at the back of the neck. In flight the black and white underside of the tail shows well.

This dove flies fast, flicking its wings as it goes. It has a loud 'coo-coooo-coo' call. It is often found near human habitation and perches in tall trees or on house tops. It feeds mainly on the ground.

The collared dove originally lived in eastern Europe but some 50 years ago began to spread westward until now it is seen in much of north-west Europe. It began breeding in Britain in 1955 and is now widespread and common. It is usually seen in pairs.

The turtle dove *S. turtur* is our smallest pigeon at 28cm long. It is a summer visitor to northern Europe and in Britain usually breeds only in the south.

On its back and wings, the turtle dove is reddish, spotted with black. At the sides of the neck are black and white striped patches. In flight the light underside is seen, plus a black tail with a large white border.

The turtle dove is a bird of woodland, hedges and semi-open country with plenty of cover.

Cuckoo

The cuckoo is usually grey with a barred breast, but some females and all juveniles show distinctive variations.

The cuckoo flies fast and low. It has a rather hawk-line outline.

A cuckoo lays up to twelve eggs a year, one in each nest. The foster-parents are much smaller species than the cuckoo, such as the robin and meadow pipit.

Cuckoos are birds with long tails and pointed wings. Perched or in flight they have a superficial resemblance to hawks. Many, including the one species that comes to western Europe, are brood parasites, they lay their eggs in the nests of other birds, which are then left to rear the cuckoo chicks.

The cuckoo *Cuculus canorus* is 33cm long including the tail. It is usually grey on head, back and wings, with the underparts white striped with grey. Most young cuckoos, and a few adult females, have a red-brown back with strong barring and lighter barred underparts.

Cuckoos are found in all parts of Britain for their brief summer breeding season. They arrive in April and leave again by late July or early August. Only the male calls 'cuckoo', the female gives a liquid trill.

The cuckoo feeds on insects, often taking large hairy caterpillars which other species find unpalatable.

45

Tawny, Barn and Little owls

The **tawny owl** has streaked brown plumage and a round face. The eyes are dark.

The **tawny owl** in flight, shows its large head and big, broad, rounded wings that permit great manoeuvrability in woodland.

Owls are nocturnal birds of prey. They have large heads, short but very flexible necks, and well-developed forward-facing eyes. Hearing is also acute in many species. The wings are large in proportion to the rest of the body, and the flight silent. Prey is grabbed by powerful talons.

The tawny owl *Strix aluco* is about 38cm long. It has a rather round face and dark eyes. It is brown with streaks and mottles. Occasional greyer individuals are seen.

Very nocturnal, the tawny owl roosts hidden in a tree by day and becomes active at dusk. It flies well on broad, rounded wings but much of its hunting is done by waiting on a branch to observe prey. It feeds mainly on voles and mice.

Although owls may be difficult to see, the tawny owl is often heard. It gives the 'tu-whit-tuwhoo' call, and often calls 'kee-wick, kee-wick'.

Tawny owls are common in all parts of Britain where there are trees, including towns and cities, where they live in parks and gardens. The tawny owl is found over most of the Continent but not in Ireland.

The barn owl *Tyto alba* is about 34cm long. It has a heart-shaped face with dark eyes. Buff-coloured above, British barn owls are white below. When seen flying, the

The **barn-owl** sometimes flies before dusk. Its flight is low and wavering, yet graceful and agile.

The **barn owl** is a light colour; the undersides are of variable colour. The feathered face is heart-shaped.

The **little owl** is very small and has a fierce appearance. It is sometimes seen active by day but generally hunts at dusk.

whole bird looks white and ghostly as it floats along. The barn owl is found over much of Europe except Scandinavia. Continental birds have buff rather than white breasts.

Barn owls do not hoot but give unearthly shrieks (hence their other name of screech owls), and 'snore' at the nest.

The species is widespread, but in few localities are they common. Numbers are declining, probably due to changes in farming practice and disappearance of suitable nest sites. They like to hunt in open country and farmland. They nest in hollow trees, ruined buildings or in lofts of barns.

The little owl *Athene noctua* is tiny, only 22cm long. It has a very compact body and rather flat head with yellow eyes. Sometimes it is seen by day, perched on a post or hunting. It has an undulating flight.

Found over most of continental Europe except Scandinavia, the little owl was introduced to Britain in 1889 and is now found in open country throughout England and Wales.

Short-eared and Long-eared owls

When a good view of a long-eared owl is obtained, the long ear-tufts and staring orange eyes identify it.

The short-eared owl has small, barely noticeable ear-tufts, and a round face with yellow eyes. It perches more horizontally than most owls.

The short-eared owl *Asio flammeus* is 38cm long. Its 'ears' are short tufts of feathers above each eye, and are usually difficult to pick out. The eyes are yellow, the face rather rounded. When standing, the stance is less upright than most owls and more like a typical bird.

This species of owl lives in open country such as moors and marshes. In Britain it breeds mainly in Scotland and northern England, but also breeds in East Anglia. In winter it may appear in other districts, especially coasts.

Short-eared owls are often active in broad daylight, quartering the countryside slowly on long wings searching for prey such as voles. In flight a dark patch can be seen under the bend of each wing.

The long-eared owl *A. otus* is 35cm long. It is not often seen as it is very nocturnal and its preferred habitat is woodland, usually coniferous, although it sometimes hunts over open country. It has long ear-tufts, often held erect, and very orange eyes separated by white feathers. It is relatively slender.

Long-eared owls are generally quiet, but they have an eerie moaning hoot. They feed largely on small mammals.

Nightjar

Nightjars have a buoyant flight on long wings. They have long tails and a rather hawk-like silhouette.

A nightjar at rest or on its nest scrape is almost invisible.

Nightjars are nocturnal birds that feed on insects. Their beaks are small but they can open the mouth to a very large bristle-fringed gape to trap insects.

The nightjar *Caprimulgus europaeus* is 28cm long, and the only member of the family to visit north-west Europe. It comes to Britain in May and remains until September.

The nightjar's patterned brown plumage makes an almost perfect camouflage as it sits on the ground or on a branch. It perches along the length of a branch rather than across it as most birds. As it rests inactive during the day and is active at night it is extremely difficult to see, but its presence may be given away by its churring song.

Sometimes the nightjar is seen at dusk chasing insects, flying on long wings, twisting and turning as it follows its prey. Male nightjars may be distinguished by white patches on the wings and tail.

Nightjars are found on heathland, dunes and among bracken and woodland edges. They are still widespread but are steadily becoming less common.

Swift

The **swift** only perches when at the nest. Its feet are small. Even when folded, the wings extend behind the body.

The **swift** looks almost black in flight. It flies very fast on long scimitar-shaped wings.

Swifts have long scimitar-shaped wings and short, forked tails. They catch insects on the wing, and of all birds are the most aerial, spending virtually all their time on the wing except when at the nest. They remain aloft at night, with intervals of cat-napping or even sleeping on currents of rising air interspersed with periods of flapping to gain height.

The swift *Apus apus* is the only species of the family to visit Britain and northern Europe. It is 17cm long and has dark brown plumage, often appearing black. It is lighter below the chin, but this can rarely be noticed.

The swift's wingspan is noticeably greater than the length of the bird. It flies very fast in an arc across the sky, wheeling to pursue swarms of flying insects. Swifts may fly very high, or at times descend to fly at house-top or even head level. As they go they give a screaming call.

Swifts can be seen in Britain during the summer. In some parts they arrive as late as May and depart as early as August. They are widespread, except in northern Scotland; they are absent from Orkney and Shetland.

Originally cliff-nesters, swifts have adopted the eaves of houses as a suitable alternative.

Kingfisher and Hoopoe

The **kingfisher** in flight is a flash of blue with whirring wings.

The kingfisher perches upright on short legs. The beak and head are large, and the colouring unlike any other British bird.

The **rarely-seen hoopoe** has barred wings, a pinkish body, and a crest that can be raised or lowered.

Kingfishers have large heads and beaks, compact bodies and short tails. Most species hunt fish and live near water. Only one species is found in western Europe.

The kingfisher *Alcedo atthis* is 17cm long. It is blue on its back and blue with a touch of green on the wings and top of the head. The breast is orange-red and there is an orange-red stripe through the eye, with a patch of white behind this, and also a white chin. It may hover when hunting, or perches on a branch overhanging the water to watch for prey. It plunges after small fish, usually returning to a perch to swallow them head first.

This colourful bird is found through most of Britain and Europe, but numbers are badly affected by cold winters. It is absent from northern Scotland and most of Scandinavia.

The hoopoe *Upupa epops* (28cm long), an ally of the kingfisher, lives in most of Europe except Scandinavia, but in Britain it is an uncommon visitor, and rare breeder, in the south only. The long bill is used in probing for grubs.

Woodpeckers

male

female

juvenile

The green woodpecker is the largest woodpecker in Britain. It has a red cap and green, grey and yellow coloration. The moustache stripe is red in males only.

The green woodpecker may be seen on the ground gathering ants.

Woodpeckers are brightly coloured birds with extremely strong sharp bills, able to hammer at trees to extract insects or make nest holes. The tongue is very long and can be protruded to seize grubs. The feet are adapted for climbing, with two toes pointing forward and two backward, all with sharp claws. These, and the stiff tail feathers, are used to support the body, and the woodpecker always climbs head-up. Woodpecker flight is extremely undulating.

The green woodpecker *Picus viridis* is 32cm long. In flight the bird looks surprisingly yellow. The green woodpecker is the one most likely to be seen on the ground as it is fond of ants, which it digs from their nests. On the ground it hops. It also climbs trees in typical woodpecker fashion. It has a loud laughing call.

This woodpecker is typically a bird of deciduous woodland, but may be seen in open conifer woods, or in open country near woodland. It is found through most of western Europe but is absent from northern Scotland, northern Scandinavia and Ireland.

The great spotted woodpecker *Dendrocopos major* is 23cm long. Black above, it has white patches on the

The **lesser spotted woodpecker** is sparrow size and has black and white bars on the wings.

The **great spotted woodpecker** is mainly black and white. The large white patch on the wings and the red under the tail are good recognition features. The male alone has a red nape.

face, on the side of the neck, and on the wings, with white barring on the outer parts of the wing feathers. The underside is greyish-white, but under the tail is a striking red patch. The male alone has red on the back of the neck, although young have a red cap.

The great spotted woodpecker is common in woodland throughout Britain and western Europe, but is not resident in Ireland or northern Scandinavia. It is the woodpecker most often heard as, in addition to drilling trees for food, it drums loudly on trees in spring to attract a mate.

The lesser spotted woodpecker *D. minor* is quite tiny at 15cm long. The male has a red cap, the female white. This woodpecker is widely distributed in western Europe, but is absent from northern Britain and from Ireland.

Waxwing and Starling

The waxwing's black face markings and striking swept-back crest are easier features to spot than the red markings that give it its name.

Waxwings are gregarious fruit-eating birds. The way they fly, and their flocking, gives them some resemblance to starlings.

The waxwing *Bombycilla garrulus* is 18cm long. It has attractive pinkish-grey plumage and darker wings. The tail has a yellow tip and is reddish below. There is black and yellow at the wing edge and the bird gets its name from the little dab of red on the wing, although this is not always very obvious in the field.

The dark eye-stripe and bib make a striking face, and the head is topped by a backward-sweeping crest, a little larger in males than females.

The normal habitat of the waxwing is the coniferous forests of northern Europe and Asia. It feeds on berries of various kinds, particularly rowan. In winter the birds move south and each year a small number visit eastern Britain. Some years the northern berry crops fail. This may send larger than normal invasions of waxwings south and west. In such 'irruption' years the number of waxwings visiting Britain in winter may be numbered in thousands rather than the usual trickle, and they go much further west. Parties of waxwings may be seen stripping berry bushes, giving their soft trilling call as they do so.

Starlings are medium-sized birds. There are many tropical species, some very colourful, but only one species is found in western Europe.

The starling in winter is more strongly spotted than in summer, but the bill is not so bright. Young starlings are rather plain, grey-brown with a lighter throat.

summer

winter

juvenile

winter

The starling is mainly dark with a glossy, coloured sheen and yellow bill in summer.

The winter plumage of the spotless starling *S. unicolor*, shown here, can easily be confused with the starling. This species is a resident of Spain and north Africa.

The starling *Sturnus vulgaris* is 21cm long. Blackish in appearance, but glossy at close quarters, it has a light speckling. The bill is quite long, yellow in the breeding season and dark in winter. The bird is alert, gregarious and sometimes quarrelsome. It stands and perches rather upright, and on the ground may hop or walk. It feeds on a variety of insects and their grubs, and on other small animals, together with some fruits and berries.

This species is very common and is found throughout Britain, from remote locations to the middle of cities. In some places starlings congregate and roost in thousands. In winter starlings leave northern and eastern Europe. Large numbers of these migrants come to the British Isles.

The starling flies fast and straight, with intermittent glides. Tight-packed flocks of thousands may fly and turn apparently in unison. In flight the starling has pointed triangular wings and a rather fan-shaped tail.

Starlings are noisy, giving a churring call and harsh squawks, as well as many sweeter sounds. They are also good mimics, both of other animals sounds and of some mechanical noises.

55

Shrikes

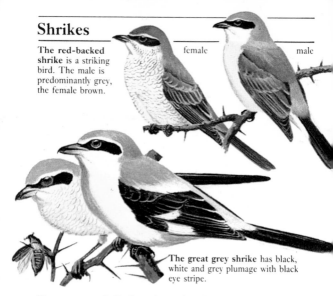

The red-backed shrike is a striking bird. The male is predominantly grey, the female brown.

female   male

The great grey shrike has black, white and grey plumage with black eye stripe.

The great grey shrike *L. excubitor* is 24cm long, the largest European shrike. It has contrasting black, white and grey plumage. The female may have faint barring on the breast. It is found by hedges, heaths and woodland edges. In Britain it is only a visitor, seen in small numbers in winter in the east.

Shrikes are medium-sized birds with carnivorous habits. They have strong bills with hooked tips and feed on insects and small birds, mammals and reptiles. They often perch in exposed positions waiting for prey, then make 'larders' by impaling them on thorns.

The red-backed shrike *Lanius collurio* is 17cm long. It is a summer visitor to warmer parts of Europe. It is becoming increasingly rare in southern Britain and nests only in the south-east. The male has striking plumage. The head and rump are grey above. The back and wings are chestnut, the tail is black, and there is a prominent black stripe through each eye above a white cheek. The breast is pale pinkish-buff. The female is not so bright, mainly red-brown above and with a pale breast with darker crescent marks. The eye-stripe is less strongly marked and in some is scarcely noticeable.

This is a bird of scrubland and open country with bushes. Its 'chack, chack' call draws attention. It flies on long pointed wings and has a long tail; it can hover. Its shape and habits give a resemblance to a small hawk.

Larks

The skylark is a small brown-streaked ground bird with a small crest.

The skylark has a long song-flight.

The woodlark has a prominent pale eye-stripe.

Larks are fairly small birds. Most have brown-streaked plumage. They live on the ground in open country and have a running gait. Their dull colours are compensated for by melodious songs, usually given on the wing. The claw on the hind toes is very long.

The skylark *Alauda arvensis* is 18cm long. It is brown with dark streaks, except on the belly, which is pale.

Skylarks are found in all sorts of open country, feeding on seeds, insects and worms. They are common throughout Europe and occur all over Britain, numbers being swollen in winter by migrants from northern Europe. Outside the breeding season skylarks may be seen in flocks, but during breeding each male defends a territory. To do this, and to attract a mate, the skylark gives a long song-flight. It rises almost vertically, hovers high in the sky, then closes its wings and plunges earthward. Throughout this performance it gives a loud melodious warbling song.

The woodlark *Lullula arborea* is 15cm long. It is found in much of western Europe but is absent from northern Britain and northern Scandinavia. In Britain it is less common than it used to be and is rather local. It lives on heaths, woodland edges and scrubland. In song-flight it circles in the air before dropping. The song is quieter than the skylark's.

Swallows and Martins

The swallow has long tail streamers. It is dark blue above, pale buff below, with a red chin.

Swallows are streamlined birds with long pointed wings and forked tails. Their bills are short but they can open their mouths wide to catch insects in flight. They rarely land on the ground, but their short legs do allow them to perch, and flocks may be seen assembled on telephone wires.

The swallow *Hirundo rustica* is 19cm long, but some of this length is accounted for by the long streamers on each side of the forked tail. It is not such a big bird as the swift, and its wings are shorter and broader. Swallows in flight may look black and white at first glance, but in fact they are steel-blue above, pale buff below, with a red throat and brow that is a good identifying feature.

This is a summer visitor to Europe, and may be seen all over Britain in places that can provide insects and suitable nest sites. The swallow builds a saucer-shaped nest of mud and dried grass, typically on a ledge or rafter in a barn or out-house, so is heavily reliant on

The house martin has a short, but strongly forked, tail. It is blue-black above and pure white below on its body.

The sand martin is small. The upperparts are all brown. The underside of the body is white, with an obvious dark brown band across the chest. It does not nest on houses.

human habitation. It is a fast, smooth flier. It often flies close to the ground over farmland, or near the surface of water.

The house martin *Delichon urbica* is 13cm long. It is blue-black above, with a bright white rump, and the body is white below with dark wings. The tail is forked but lacks streamers like the swallow's. Its flight is less flowing than the swallow's, but it may go quite high.

House martins are also summer visitors. Most nest under the eaves of houses, but some build their enclosed mud-cup nests on cliffs. Large numbers may occur together.

The sand martin *Riparia riparia* is 12cm long, the smallest of this family to summer in Europe. It is brown above, white below, with a dark band across the chest and dark underwings. Sand martins are very gregarious and are often seen feeding over water. They have a rather erratic flight. They nest in colonies, boring tunnels in banks of rivers, sand or gravel pits, or in cliffs.

Pipits

The meadow pipit is a slender, small, streaked bird. The outer tail feathers are characteristically white.

The rock pipit has dark outer tail feathers, and is largely confined to rocky coasts.

These are small ground-living birds of open country. They walk or run. They are streaked brown and are rather slender with long tails.

The meadow pipit *Anthus pratensis* is 15cm long. It is the commonest pipit to be seen in Britain, where it is resident, and is also found on the Continent, but only as a summer visitor in the north. It is dark on the back, with streaks, and has a pale front, also streaked. It has a rather long tail with white outer feathers that show as it flies away. It has a rather jerky flight.

Meadow pipits are found in all sorts of open country, from grassland to moors and coasts.

The rock pipit *A. spinoletta* is 17cm long. It is found on the western seaboard of continental Europe and in Britain. It is larger and darker than the meadow pipit. It also has darker legs and rather dark outer tail feathers. As its name suggests, the rock pipit is found near rocks and is largely a bird of rocky coasts, although other types of coast may be visited in winter.

Wagtails

The pied wagtail occurs only in Britain and some of the nearby coasts on the Continent. The usual form on the Continent is the white wagtail, which is the same species but has a grey back. This form occasionally visits Britain.

The yellow wagtail is mainly yellow and has a relatively short tail. The Continental form of the same species is the blue-headed wagtail in which males have a blue-grey head.

Wagtails are slender birds that spend much of their time on the ground, where they walk or run. Their legs are relatively long and thin, and they have long tails that are continually bobbed and give them their name. They are brightly patterned, and are often seen close to water.

The pied wagtail *Motacilla alba* is 18cm long. In summer the male is white on his face and underside, and black above with a black bib and neck. The female is greyer, with less bib. In winter both sexes are grey on the back and the black bib does not reach under the chin. The pied wagtail can catch insects in the air and may be seen jumping up and catching food. It has a very undulating flight. It is common in farmland and open country, and nests in holes in rocks or buildings.

The yellow wagtail *M. flava* is 16.5cm long, and has a shorter tail than the pied wagtail. It is mainly yellow, with greenish-brown above. It is seen on meadows and marshes. It is a summer visitor that breeds throughout England but is absent from most of the rest of the British Isles.

Crows, Rook and Raven

These are large perching birds with powerful bills. The plumage is generally black. Their voices tend to be harsh. Some species are gregarious.

The carrion crow *Corvus corone* is 46cm long. The plumage is all black, slightly glossy at close quarters, and the feathers extend to the base of the thick beak. The crow is most likely to be seen singly or in small groups. In flight, it shows broad wings with separated wingtips and a rather square tail. It flies with slow, regular wingbeats, but sometimes appears to drift sideways. The crow occurs throughout Britain and Europe, typically in open country, but is seen in most places, including cities.

There are two colour forms of this species. Through western Europe and in Britain right up into Scotland the all-black carrion crow is seen. In Scandinavia, eastern Europe, Ireland and north-west Scotland the usual crow is the hooded crow. In places the two forms live alongside one another and may interbreed.

The crow is very adaptable and feeds on all kinds of food from grain and fruits, through snails, insects, worms, frogs and eggs, to nestlings and carrion. On the ground it usually walks, with a slight waddle.

The rook *C. frugilegus* is 46cm long. About the same size as the crow, its beak looks longer and more pointed, and there is a grey patch of bare skin at its base. The feathers at the top of the legs are rather loose, and give a baggy-trousered effect. At close quarters a purple gloss can be seen on the black plumage.

Rooks are very sociable, nesting in colonies in trees, and flying and feeding in flocks. In flight the wings beat faster than the crow's. A 'caw' is the usual call. Rooks are common in farmland, where they find food in the fields and nest in groups of trees. They live throughout Britain and north-west Europe, but not northern Scandinavia.

The raven *C. corax* is the largest of the crows at 64cm. It is essentially a bird of relatively undisturbed places, so in Britain is usually seen in upland and moorland areas. It lives in suitable places throughout the Northern Hemisphere.

On the wing the raven is a good acrobat in spite of its size. It often soars and glides as it searches for carrion. The tail is wedge-shaped. The voice is a deep croak.

The rook has a narrow pointed bill, a bare patch at the base of the bill, and baggy 'trousers'.

The carrion crow on the wing has broad wings and a square tail.

The carrion crow is black. It has a strong bill.

The hooded crow has a grey back and breast. This colour variant is seen in northern Scotland.

The raven is huge, with a powerful bill and a 'beard'. In flight the tail is wedge-shaped.

Jay, Magpie and Jackdaw

The jay *Garrulus glandarius* is 34cm long. It is brightly patterned. Most of the body is pinkish-brown, but the tail is black and there is a vivid white rump patch. The wings have black and white markings and there is a 'shoulder' patch of blue feathers. The bill and 'moustache' are black, and the black-streaked feathers on top of the head can be raised into a small crest that gives the head a square look. The eyes are blue.

This is an alert, restless bird, and in spite of its colouring it is not always easy to get a good view of it in its woodland surroundings. As it flies away, the white rump patch and the white on the wings are noticeable. The flight is rather slow and jerky. The jay gives a loud 'skaark, skaark' alarm call that may give away its presence. It will eat all kinds of food, from berries, to grubs and the eggs and chicks of other birds. In autumn it may be seen burying acorns for later use.

Jays are found through most of Europe, but do not reach northern Scotland or northern Scandinavia.

The magpie *Pica pica* is up to 46cm long, of which half is tail. The long tail and black and white plumage (the black is glossy blue and green at close quarters) make the magpie easy to identify. Its flight is slow, but the wingbeats are quite fast, interspersed with glides. The long tail and short rounded wings give a distinctive silhouette.

On the ground the magpie walks with the tail up and sometimes hops. It feeds on a variety of insects, seeds and fruit, and has a bad name as a robber of other bird's eggs and young. It is common throughout Europe on farmland and in open country with trees and hedges.

The jackdaw *Corvus monedula* is 33cm long. Its small size and grey feathers on the neck and sides of the face identify this mainly black bird.

Found throughout Europe, except for northern Scandinavia, the jackdaw is found in fairly open country, including farmland, parks and coasts with cliffs. It nests, often in colonies, in cavities in trees, cliffs and buildings, sometimes using chimneys.

The jackdaw flies well, with fairly fast wingbeats, and may be seen, especially by cliffs, soaring and doing aerobatics. It walks with a strutting action, and its call is a high-pitched 'jack'. It is often seen in flocks.

The **jay** has blue feathers on the wing and blue eyes. Most of the body is pinkish-brown. Sometimes the head feathers are raised.

The **jay** in flight displays its white rump and white wing-patches.

The **magpie** in flight is rather moth-like, slow but with fast wingbeats.

The **magpie's** black and white plumage and long tail make it easy to identify.

The **jackdaw's** grey neck contrasts with the black cap of the head. Much of the time it is a gregarious bird.

Dipper

The **dipper** flies fast and low.

The **dipper's** dumpy shape, white breast, and habit of bobbing, make it an easy bird to recognize.

juvenile

Dippers have strong legs and are wren-like in shape. They are found by water, usually strongly flowing streams.

The dipper *Cinclus cinclus* is 18cm long. A dumpy bird with a short cocked-up tail and sturdy legs, it is found throughout Europe and northern Asia, usually near fast-flowing hill streams. In Britain, therefore, it is seen in the north and west.

Adult dippers of both sexes are mainly brown, but the throat is a conspicuous white. Young birds are a dull grey. Dippers get their name from the bobbing action of the body when they are perched on a rock. They obtain their food from the water, eating tiny fish, water beetles and other larval and adult insects. They are able to wade, swim or dive for food. Most remarkably, the dipper is able to walk underwater upstream searching for food, using the force of the stream against its partly-spread wings to counteract its natural buoyancy.

The dipper flies fast and low, usually keeping over water. Its call is a short metallic note.

Wren

The wren has a tiny body but a loud voice. Its quick movements, fast whirring flight and cocked-up tail help to confirm its identity.

Wrens are small, rather round birds with a cocked-up tail when perching and restless habits.

The wren *Troglodytes troglodytes* is 9.5cm long. It is dark reddish-brown above, rather lighter below, and is closely barred on the wings, tail and sides.

Wrens are very active, poking among ground litter for food and also picking food from the leaves. They feed on small insects and spiders. They live in undergrowth, low vegetation and rocks in a wide variety of habitats from gardens to mountains. They are found through most of Europe; the wren is possibly Britain's commonest bird.

The wren's voice is surprisingly loud for so small a bird. The call is a sharp 'tit-tit-tit'. The song is fast and shrill.

The wren is one of the few British birds to build a domed nest. It is built by the male, who may build several before the female chooses one in which to lay. The nest is made in a bush or hollow in a wall and comprises moss, leaves and grass. The nestlings are fed by both parents.

Because of their small size, wrens are vulnerable to cold weather. Sometimes several will squeeze into the same cavity in winter to roost and keep warm.

Dunnock, Blackcap and Whitethroat

The dunnock is a dull-coloured self-effacing bird that keeps to cover or to the ground. The plumage, streaked brown above and grey below, looks smart at close quarters.

male

female

The blackcap male lives up to its name, but the female has a reddish-brown cap.

The Accentor family to which the dunnock belongs comprises superficially sparrow-like birds with brownish plumage. Unlike sparrows they are chiefly insect feeders, and have thin, sharp bills. Their quiet plumage and quiet habits make them easily overlooked.

The dunnock *Prunella modularis* is 14.5cm long. It is streaked brown above and plain grey below. It is very unobtrusive, keeping in cover or close to it. On the ground it hops along, with frequent pauses, in a rather low crouched attitude, twitching its wings frequently as it searches for food. It sings nearly all year a short, thin tinkling song. It also calls insistently a squeaky 'tseep'.

The dunnock is found through much of western Europe, and is resident through all of the British Isles. It leaves Scandinavia and eastern Europe in winter. It has the distinction in southern Britain of being probably the most frequent host for the cuckoo.

Warblers are, like accentors, small birds, mostly rather dull in colour. They are insect-eaters with

male

female

The whitethroat has a white throat and reddish-brown wings. There are slight differences of shade between the sexes.

slender pointed bills. Many are rather active in habit.

Many species of warbler are rather similar in appearance, making identification difficult when only brief glimpses are caught, but most have distinctive songs that no doubt help them, as well as humans, to identify their own species.

The blackcap *Sylvia atricapilla* is 14cm long. It is one of the few warblers in which male and female are obviously different. The male has a black cap, the female has a red-brown cap. Both are otherwise greyish-brown above, lighter below. The blackcap is a summer visitor to northern Europe. In Britain it does not usually reach northern Scotland. A few birds overwinter in Britain.

This species likes wooded areas, including parks and gardens. The male has a melodious song, often given from within a thicket. The bird keeps within cover much of the time, and makes short jerky flights between one patch of bushes and the next.

The whitethroat *S. communis* is 14cm long. It has brown wings and the body is greyish-brown above, lighter below. Both sexes have a white throat, but the male has a greyer head than the female. The long tail is white-edged. The whitethroat is a summer visitor to Europe, and may be seen throughout Britain in scrub, hedges, commons and woodland clearings. It has a scolding call, and the song is delivered in a short dancing flight.

Goldcrest

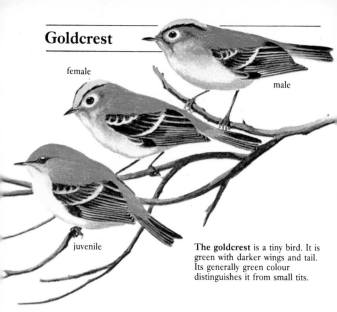

female

male

juvenile

The goldcrest is a tiny bird. It is green with darker wings and tail. Its generally green colour distinguishes it from small tits.

The goldcrest *Regulus regulus* is only 9cm long, the smallest British bird. It is resident throughout Britain and most of western Europe.

The goldcrest is tiny, but plump-looking, with a small thin bill. The general body colour is yellowish-green, lighter below, with darker wings and tail. Along the crown of the head is a yellow stripe (sometimes showing orange in the male) bordered with black.

Goldcrests are especially fond of conifers, but may sometimes be seen in deciduous woods or hedgerows. They spend much time high in the trees but if they come low they may go about their business apparently unconcerned by a close human presence. Goldcrests are busy little birds that work their way through the trees picking off small insects and spiders with their tiny pointed beaks. The call is a high, shrill 'zee-zee-zee'.

Out of the breeding season, goldcrests sometimes join feeding parties of tits but goldcrests look small by comparison. In the breeding season the males are very aggressive to one another. The goldcrest's nest is a 'hammock' built and slung below the end of a branch of a conifer tree and is woven from spiders webs, moss and feathers.

Willow and Sedge warblers

The willow warbler is greenish above, yellowish below, with a stripe above each eye. It is a restless bird.

The sedge warbler is common in waterside vegetation. Juveniles may have a faintly spotted breast.

The willow warbler *Phylloscopus trochilus* is 11cm long. It is common throughout northern Europe including Britain, in summer, but migrates south for the winter. It is by no means confined to willows, being found in woods of all kinds, scrub, hedges and open areas with patches of trees. It lives mainly, but not exclusively, in the lower storeys of vegetation. It is greenish above, yellowish below, and usually has pale legs. A pale stripe runs just above each eye. Another warbler, the chiffchaff, looks almost identical, but has a very different song and usually lives higher in woodland.

The sedge warbler *Acrocephalus schoenobaenus* is 12.5cm long. It lives in beds of reeds and other swamp vegetation along the edges of rivers and lakes. It has dark, streaked upperparts and is lighter below. Above each eye is a very distinct pale stripe. It may be heard singing its varied song from a perch or during the short, vertical song flight. The sedge warbler visits Europe including most suitable areas of the British Isles, from April to September.

Flycatchers

female

male

The pied flycatcher male has very bold plumage but the female is a more muted brown.

The spotted flycatcher is slightly streaked, but basically a rather nondescript colour. Its habit of flying up to catch an insect and returning to the same perch help identify it.

Flycatchers are small birds with small bills and large gapes that catch insects by making a short darting flight from a perch. They sit rather upright on their vantage point watching for prey.

The spotted flycatcher *Muscicapa striata* is 14cm long and does not have spots. It is brown above with a slightly streaked head, and paler below with some streaking on the breast. The sexes are the same. It is a summer visitor to Europe and is found all over the British Isles in gardens, parkland and open woods. The spotted flycatcher makes repeated flights from the same perch, chasing insects with a twisting, fluttering flight.

The pied flycatcher *Ficedula hypoleuca* is 13cm long. The male is black and white, the female brown and white, as is the male after the breeding season. Both sexes have a white wing patch and white edges to the tail.

A summer visitor to northern Europe, the pied flycatcher is mainly seen in the west and north of Britain, but does not get to northern Scotland. It is mainly a bird of deciduous woodland, often found in valleys in hilly areas. It may feed high in the trees and does not usually return to the same perch after catching an insect.

Wheatear and Whinchat

male

The **wheatear** is seen in open country.

female

Both sexes have a white rump and a tail that is black down the centre and back, but with white edges.

male

Whinchats are often seen perched on low bushes in rough country giving their 'teck teck' call.

juvenile

female

The wheatear *Oenanthe oenanthe* is 14.5cm long. It is a summer visitor to Europe. In Britain it is found chiefly in the north and west and is now rare in south-east and central England. It lives on downs, hill pastures, moors and seaside grassland. It nests in holes, sometimes in rabbit burrows. It feeds largely on insects.

The male wheatear has a grey back and crown and a black eye-stripe with white surround. The female is brown above and across each eye.

The whinchat *Saxicola rubetra* is 13cm long. It is a summer visitor and can be found in suitable habitat throughout Britain. It lives in rough open country with bushes and may be seen on moors, by coasts, on grassland and on commons where there are gorse and other bushes. It often perches upright on a low bush. It sings from this position but feeds mostly on the ground. Dark brown above, buff below, the whinchat has a pale stripe above each eye. The male is more brightly marked than the female. Both sexes have white on the sides of the tail but not on the rump.

Robin and Redstart

The redstart has, in both sexes, a reddish tail which is constantly jerked.

male

female

The robin is a familiar jaunty bird with a red breast.

juvenile

The robin *Erithacus rubecula* is 14cm long and such a familiar bird with its orange-red face and breast that it is unlikely to be mistaken for anything else. Both male and female are red-breasted but the young birds are speckled. All share a plump shape and lack an obvious neck.

Robins are resident throughout Europe except northern Scandinavia but only in Britain are they characteristically tame. They are birds of the undergrowth and are found in gardens, parks and woods. They perch rather upright and may flick their wings and tail. They usually fly low, with whirring wings, and not very far. They feed largely on the ground. They sing from a prominent perch to proclaim a territory.

The redstart *Phoenicurus phoenicurus* is 14cm long. Its name means red-tail and the red-brown tail is prominent as it is frequently jerked up and down. The female is otherwise rather dull but the male has a black throat and face with a white brow, a grey back and chestnut breast. The redstart is seen in open woodland, parks and gardens. It is a summer visitor to Europe, including Britain but not Ireland.

Nightingale and Bluethroat

The nightingale is an inconspicuous bird more likely to be heard than seen.

male

female

juvenile

The bluethroat is a rare visitor to Britain. Males in breeding plumage are unmistakable.

The nightingale *Luscinia megarhynchos* is 16.5cm long and rather dull to look at. It is a summer visitor to Europe but does not reach Scandinavia and in Britain is found only in the south-east. It lives in deciduous woodland with thickets and plentiful undergrowth. It is a shy bird and difficult to see as it hides away in cover for much of the time. Its song draws attention to it; it is loud, varied and musical. The nightingale sings by day and night, usually concealed in a thicket, feeding on the ground on insects and other small animals. It builds its nest low down, well-hidden.

The bluethroat *L. svecica* is a robin-sized bird 14cm long. It is a summer visitor to much of Asia and reaches Scandinavia and parts of western Europe but is only a rare visitor to Britain, usually at the time of autumn migration. Females are rather inconspicuous but the reddish tail-patches show as the tail is frequently flicked. Males have a blue throat underlined by black and chestnut. In Scandinavian males in the middle of the blue is a reddish spot. In southern Europe the spot is white.

Blackbird, Ring ouzel and Song thrush

The **blackbird** is a familiar garden bird. The male is black with a bright yellow beak. The female is dark brown, sometimes slightly spotted below.

male

female

male

female

The **ring ouzel** has a white collar, more developed in the male. It is a bird of moors and mountain.

The blackbird *Turdus merula* is 25cm long. The male is black all over with a yellow bill. The female is dark brown with a brownish bill; it may look quite uniform or have ill-defined spots on the lighter underside. Sometimes albino or partly albino specimens are seen.

This is a bird of woodland edges and glades that has found man's gardens very much to its taste. It nests and rests in bushes, but does much of its feeding on the ground. Noisy scufflings in the leaf litter as it looks for insects and worms often draw attention. It searches for worms on lawns, often pausing with its head cocked.

The blackbird has got a loud alarm call. It also has a strong fluting song. It is one of Britain's commonest birds. It is a resident here and over most of Europe, but it does not reach northern Scandinavia.

The **song thrush** is brown above and spotted below in both sexes. It has a loud musical song in which phrases are repeated.

The **song thrush** flies fast and straight, showing buff patches beneath the front of the wings.

The **song thrush** cracks snails on a stone before eating the soft parts.

The ring ouzel *T. torquatus* is 24cm long, just smaller than the blackbird, which it resembles. It is found on high moorland and mountains and is a summer visitor to northern Europe and Britain. It has a broad white collar on the upper part of its breast, more obvious in the black male than in the duller female. There is also a greyish patch on the wing. Ring ouzels fly fast. They are shy and difficult to approach.

The song thrush *T. philomelos* is 23cm long. It is brown above, whitish-buff below, with dark brown spots on the breast. Like the blackbird it is an alert-looking bird that is as much at home in gardens as in woodlands and parks.

This thrush is found through much of Europe, but migrates away from the east and north in winter. In Britain it is resident, but additional birds arrive from the Continent in winter. The song thrush has a fine voice and it sings through much of the year. It feeds on fruits and berries, insects, some worms, and especially snails, which it holds in its beak and smashes on an 'anvil' stone to get at the soft body.

77

Redwing, Fieldfare and Mistle thrush

The redwing has a dark back and reddish flanks. It is speckled below and there is a white stripe above each eye.

The redwing in flight shows the patch beneath the forewings that gives it its name.

The redwing *Turdus iliacus* is only 21cm long, the smallest European thrush. It nests from Scandinavia eastward. Further south, including Britain, it occurs as a winter visitor, although a few have begun to nest in Scotland.

This species has a brown back and spotted breast rather like the song thrush, but it has a white line above each eye and reddish flanks. When it flies the flanks and red underwings are obvious.

Outside the breeding season the redwing is gregarious and large flocks may be seen, sometimes in company with fieldfares. Although a woodland bird in the breeding season, in the winter redwings may often be seen on farmland, playing fields and other open areas. They obtain much of their food from on the ground, or probing into it, and prolonged frost makes survival difficult for them.

The fieldfare *T. pilaris* is 25cm long. Like the redwing it is normally only a winter visitor to Britain, although it nests further south in Europe. A few fieldfares have nested in northern Britain. It is much larger than the redwing, with which it sometimes associates. It also has a distinctive pattern, with a grey head and rump, and a chestnut back. The breast is spotted, and the tail almost black.

Fieldfares feed on wild fruit, garden berries, earthworms, snails and the occasional insect. They frequent all kinds of rough open country but can also be seen on farmland, marshes and large parks.

The mistle thrush *T. viscivorus* is 28cm long, the largest

The fieldfare has a grey head and rump. The back is chestnut and the tail dark.

The mistle thrush is large and has well-defined spots, and a rather greyer back than the song thrush.

of our thrushes. It is grey-brown above and on the breast the spots are round and bold. When it flies it shows the white underside of the wings. The outer tail feathers have white tips. The mistle thrush is resident throughout most of Europe, but leaves Scandinavia and north-east Europe in winter. It is found in woods, parks and gardens in the breeding season. Out of the breeding season it may be encountered in small parties in open country.

The mistle thrush stands more erect than other thrushes. In flight it frequently closes its wings, but flies strongly. It is fond of fruits and berries, including those of the mistletoe that gives it its name. It also feeds on worms, insects and snails, but does not use an anvil like the song thrush.

Mistle thrushes sing from the treetop. Even in some of the worst weather their voices may be heard. For this reason they have the country name of 'stormcock'.

Tits 1

The **blue tit** has a blue cap, wings and tail. The white face has black markings round it, and the belly is yellow.

The **coal tit** is small and has a white patch at the back of the neck. The cheeks are white, the rest of the head black. The upperparts of the body are green-grey and the underparts pale.

Tits are small plump birds with short bills and acrobatic feeding habits. Most have striking markings and the sexes are similar. Some species become very tame, and they are frequent visitors to bird tables. Most are hole-nesters so can be attracted to nest boxes. Tits have an undulating flight.

The blue tit *Parus caeruleus* is 11.5cm long. It has a blue cap and a white face. Below the beak, round the neck and in a stripe through each eye, it is black. The wings and tail are blue and the underside is yellow.

Blue tits are found as residents throughout Europe, except northern Scandinavia, in woodlands and gardens. They are alert, active little birds. They climb all over trees searching out insects, and may often be seen hanging upside-down. When they fly they have a rather bouncing, jerky action and seldom make long flights.

During the winter blue tits often join mixed feeding parties with other kinds of tit and some other small birds. They can become very confident and tame and are favourites at the bird table. They are probably the most frequent occupants of garden nestboxes, where they rear

The great tit is larger and has a heavier build than the other tits. It has a black cap, neck and bib, which continues in a black stripe down the middle of the yellow belly.

broods of up to fifteen young. They are adept at using artificial feeders of various kinds and in some areas have learned to take the cream from milk-bottles on doorsteps.

The coal tit *P. ater* is 11cm long, a little smaller than the blue tit. It has a black crown and bib, with white on the cheeks and a noticeable white patch at the back of the neck. The breast is pale and the back and tail are dingy green-grey. On the wings two white bars can be picked out. The coal tit is found through most of Europe. It is a woodland bird, preferring conifers, but also to be seen in other types of wood. It often hunts up tree trunks.

The great tit *P. major* is 14cm long. It is found throughout Europe and in Britain is a common resident in woodlands and gardens. It has a greenish back and yellow belly. The cheeks are white. The rest of the head is black and a black stripe runs from the throat down on the belly. It has a great variety of calls. In spring its insistent, ringing, 'teacher-teacher-teacher' call is most frequently heard.

The great tit is an intelligent bird and shows great ingenuity in getting at food in awkward situations.

The long-tailed tit has a tail longer than its body. It is black and white with a pinkish tinge to the plumage. The head is white with dark stripes over the eyes in western European individuals, but lacking stripes in Scandinavia.

The long-tailed tit builds an elaborate ovoid domed nest.

The long-tailed tit *Aegithalos caudatus* is 14cm long, but more than half is tail, so the round body is quite tiny. It has a rather pinkish plumage with black and white markings. The long tail is black. The cap of the head is white, with black stripes just above each eye. (In Scandinavia the head is completely white.)

This tit is resident throughout Europe. In Britain it is nearly everywhere except some parts of Scotland. It lives in hedges, thickets and woodland edges and clearings. Sometimes it is seen on scrubland or heath with bushes. It does not commonly come to small gardens or visit bird-tables.

In winter long-tailed tits keep to the shelter of woods and stay in family parties that may join mixed tit flocks. They huddle together when roosting to keep warm.

Long-tailed tits build a domed nest in the fork of a tree, using cobwebs, hair and moss and covering it with lichens and lining it with great quantities of feathers.

The marsh tit *Parus palustris* is 11.5cm long. It has a

The marsh tit has a brown back and black cap. It is to be seen in woodland rather than marshes.

The crested tit has a prominent black and white speckled crest. It can only be seen in a restricted area of Britain.

glossy black cap and grey-brown upperparts. It is paler below. It is not especially fond of marshes. Its typical habitat is deciduous woodland, especially oak, where there is undergrowth. It may visit hedgerows and parks. It is found on the Continent as far north as southern Scandinavia. In Britain it is found in England and Wales, but scarcely penetrates into Scotland.

The willow tit looks almost identical to the marsh tit and has a similar range in Britain. It has a dull, rather than glossy cap, and is fond of damp woodlands.

The crested tit *P. cristatus* is 11.5cm long. It has a speckled black and white crest above a white face with black markings. The body is brown above, pale below. The species is resident over a wide range on the Continent but in Britain it is confined to the eastern Highlands of Scotland, where it lives in conifer woods, especially pine. It searches crevices in bark for insects and eats some conifer seeds. It is more solitary than many of the tit species.

Nuthatch and Treecreeper

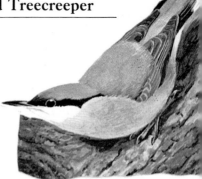

The **nuthatch** is the only European bird that habitually climbs downward head-first. It has blue-grey upper parts, buff underparts and black eye-stripes.

The **treecreeper** is easily overlooked, as it quietly climbs tree trunks in a jerky mouse-like fashion. It has a long thin bill and is brown above, white below.

Nuthatches are small birds with large heads and strong beaks. They have short legs and large feet and are good at climbing.

The nuthatch *Sitta europaea* is 14cm long. When climbing it grips with its feet alone and can climb downward head-first. The nuthatch is found over most of Europe but not in Scandinavia, nor does it go as far north as Scotland in Britain. It lives in mature woodlands and parks and gardens with large trees.

The nuthatch feeds on insects as well as various nuts. It wedges nuts in the bark of trees and hammers them with the beak to break them open. They are usually left in position so the nuthatch has to find a new crevice for each nut.

Treecreepers are small restless birds with long, thin, downcurved bills. They pick small insects and spiders from crevices in tree trunks.

The treecreeper *Certhia familiaris* is 12.5cm long, streaked brown above, and white below. It is found over much of northern Europe including the British Isles. It lives on mature trees, spiralling up the trunk as it climbs searching for food, looking rather mouse-like. From the top of the trunk it flies to the base of the next tree.

Sparrows

female

male

The house sparrow has the two sexes differently coloured. The male is a richer colour, with grey crown, black bib and chestnut shoulders.

The tree sparrow has the two sexes similarly coloured. It has a chestnut crown, white cheek patches and a small black bib.

The house sparrow *Passer domesticus* is 15cm long. It is resident throughout Europe and is closely associated with man. It can occur in all types of habitat but it is nearly always close to human habitation.

The male house sparrow has a grey crown. In front of the eyes it is black and a black bib extends down the throat on to the grey-fawn breast. It is reddish-brown round the back of the head and on the shoulders, otherwise streaky brown above. The female lacks the black throat, is generally duller, and has a pale stripe above the eye.

House sparrows are noisy and gregarious, and feed on almost anything edible in town, gardens and fields.

The tree sparrow *P. montanus* is 14cm long, a little smaller than the house sparrow. Both sexes are the same. It has a chestnut crown and white cheeks on each of which is a black spot. The bib is smaller than on the cock house sparrow.

Resident through Europe, but scarce in some parts of western Britain, the tree sparrow lives in woodland and parks in the breeding season, but flocks may be seen in open country in winter. It sometimes mixes with house sparrows, but generally is more rural in its habits.

Finches 1

The **chaffinch** in flight shows two white bars on each wing, the front one quite extensive.

male winter

male

female

The **chaffinch male** is a striking bird in the breeding season with its blue-grey cap and pinkish-brown breast. The female is duller, mainly olive-brown. Both sexes show two white wing-bars and white edges to the tail.

Finches are small seed-eating birds with short, strong bills.

The chaffinch *Fringilla coelebs* is 15cm long. It is one of Europe's commonest birds. It is resident throughout the British Isles. Numbers are boosted in winter by migrants from northern Europe.

Chaffinches are found in woods, hedgerows, gardens and on farmland, anywhere they can find bushes and trees for nesting. In winter they form flocks on fields, sometimes mixing with other species. Chaffinch winter flocks may be of one sex only. Chaffinches feed largely on the ground on seeds, hopping along with tail down. In late winter they start singing to demarcate territories. The short vigorous song ends in a flourish 'choo-ee-oo'.

The bullfinch *Pyrrhula pyrrhula* is 14.5cm long, but appears quite big, perhaps because of its striking colours and chunky silhouette. There is little 'neck' and the top of the head follows the line of the short, heavy bill. In both sexes the black cap extends to the base of the bill. Both sexes have a white rump, which shows clearly in the undulating flight.

Bullfinches are nearly always seen in pairs and they are said to mate for life. As well as seeds and berries, they feed on fruit tree buds in spring. This makes them unpopular with some growers. They are generally rather shy birds that keep near thick cover in woodland edges, hedgerows and gardens. Bullfinches are resident

The bullfinch has a silhouette and colouring that are easy to recognize. As they usually travel in pairs, it is worth looking for the duller female if a male is noticed.

The linnet is a good songster. Only the breeding male has a crimson crown and breast. The female is dull, streaked brown. Both sexes have a forked tail with white edges and white patches on the wings.

male

female

through most of western Europe, including the British Isles.

The linnet *Acanthis cannabina* is 13cm long. Both sexes have a white patch on the wings and the tail has white sides and is slightly forked.

This finch is found on heathland, common and other open places dotted with bushes and trees. It has a rather dancing flight, and is constantly calling and singing. Outside the breeding season it is very gregarious.

Linnets are found through most of Europe but move away from the north in winter. In Britain they are present all year.

Finches 2

juvenile   male   female

The yellowhammer male is
bright lemon yellow on its face
and breast. The female is duller.
Both sexes have a prominent chestnut rump.

The yellowhammer *Emberiza citrinella* is 16.5cm long.
The male looks very bright with face, underparts and
inner underwings, all lemon yellow. The face is somewhat
streaked. The female is more streaked with brown and
generally duller. Both sexes have a chestnut rump, and
this, and the white feathers at the tail's edge, are
prominent as the bird retreats. Yellowhammers have
relatively long tails and wings.

The species is resident throughout most of western
Europe. It is a bird of farmland and hedgerows,
commons and young plantations. It rarely enters gardens.
It feeds on the ground but is often seen perched on top
of a hedge or telegraph pole. From such a vantage point
it delivers its rather monotonous song, supposed to
resemble 'a-little-bit-of-bread-and-no-cheese'. Its call,
often given on the wing, is a metallic 'twink'.

The greenfinch *Carduelis chloris* is 14cm long. It is a
fairly plump finch with a powerful beak. It has long
wings and a short forked tail. The male is olive-green
with yellow and black on the wings and tail. The green
is somewhat variable. Females are much duller, but show
a similar wing and tail pattern.

The greenfinch is a resident over most of Europe
including the British Isles. It is often seen near human
habitation and is fond of gardens, parks and shrubberies,

Glossary

call A single note or a short sequence of notes given by a bird by which it signals its presence or conveys other information to others of its kind.

camouflage Colouring and behaviour that allows an animal to escape detection.

carnivorous Feeding on other animals.

carrion Decaying flesh of an animal, which may have died of natural causes or been killed by a predator.

colony A group of birds of the same kind that are breeding in the same area.

display A ritual pattern of behaviour used in courtship, aggression, etc.

distribution The geographical area in which a species is found.

drake A male duck.

eclipse plumage A dull plumage assumed out of the breeding season. Used particularly of male ducks.

feral Describes wild animals whose ancestors were domesticated individuals.

forage Search for food.

frontal On the front of the head, on the brow.

glide To fly without flapping the wings.

gregarious Living together in large groups.

habitat The type of countryside in which an animal lives.

incubate To sit on eggs or young to keep them warm.

introduction An animal not originally native to an area but that has been allowed to escape or deliberately released in it.

migrate Move from one country to another as the seasons change. Many birds breed in one part of the world and migrate to a different part at the end of the breeding season.

moult The loss of feathers. In most birds the moult is gradual and regular moults occur with the seasons. Chicks moult as they become adults.

nocturnal Active at night rather than during the day.

parasite An animal that uses another in a way that benefits the first and makes the other worse off, but without killing it. Most parasitic relationships are feeding ones, but in some birds one species uses another to bring up its young, e.g. cuckoo.

plumage The feather covering of a bird.

population The number of individuals of a particular species or a recognizable group within a species, for

This finch lives in open country with trees and bushes, scrub, waste ground, gardens and roadsides. It feeds on weed seeds and is particularly fond of thistles. It climbs all over the thistles, extracting seeds with its sharp beak. The goldfinch is resident over most of western Europe but is absent from northern Scandinavia. In the British Isles it is absent from northern Scotland.

The goldfinch *C. carduelis* is a small finch 12cm long, in which both sexes are brightly coloured. The wing-bars show well when the goldfinch flies.

visitor to bird-tables, where it is apt to throw its weight around with other birds.

and cultivated land. It nests in bushes, sometimes in close proximity to other greenfinches. It is a frequent

The goldfinch has a dancing flight that reveals the large yellow area on each wing.

The goldfinch has a red face and wide yellow wing-bars. Both sexes share the same bright pattern.

juvenile

The greenfinch has a forked tail with a characteristic pattern. The male can be a bright olive green with yellow patches. Females are much duller.

female

male

example, all the individuals within a certain area.

prey The victim of a hunting animal.

resident Present continuously in an area.

roost Perching for the night *or* group of birds that perches for the night.

scavenge To feed on carrion and other refuse.

seasonal movement A general movement made seasonally. Migration is an extreme type of seasonal movement. Many birds make less far-ranging but consistent movements, for example, living in a different habitat in winter to that used in summer, although both may be in the same country.

silhouette The outline of an object.

soar To fly without flapping wings, particularly using air currents to stay aloft over the same area.

song A sequence of notes, sometimes complex and often tuneful, used by a bird to attract a mate or show its ownership of a territory.

species Individuals characterized by a common set of features and capable of breeding, one with another, to produce fertile offspring.

talons The claws of a bird of prey.

territory An area defended by an individual or pair of birds against others of the same species. The area is usually that used for breeding purposes.

Acknowledgements

Artworks © Golden Pleasure Books, 10, 13, 14 (bottom), 15, 16, 18 (top), 19 (top), 20, 22 (top), 23, 24, 25, 26 (top), 27, 28 (centre), 29 (top left and bottom), 30, 31, 32, 33 (top left and bottom right), 34, 35 (centre right), 36, 37, 40, 41 (top left), 42 (right), 43 (left) 44 (top right and bottom left), 45, 46 (right), 47, 48, 49, 50, 51, 52, 53, 55, 56, 57, 63, 64, 66, 68 (bottom), 69, 70, 71, 72, 73, 74, 75, 77, 78, 80, 81, 82, 83, 84, 85, 86, 87, 89. Artist – Arthur Singer. Cover: John M. Davies.

Artworks © RSPB 11, 12, 14 (top), 17, 18 (bottom), 19 (bottom), 21, 22 (bottom), 26 (bottom), 28 (top and bottom), 29 (top right), 33 (top right and bottom left), 35 (top and bottom), 38, 39, 41 (top right), 42 (right), 43 (right), 44 (top left and bottom right), 46 (left) 58, 59, 60, 61, 68 (top), 76, 79. Artist – Noel Cusa.

Photographs NHPA – P. Scott 16; Frank Lane – D. Zingel 20, Wildlife Studies Ltd. 25, Aquila Photographics – W.S. Paton 36, NHPA – S. Dalton 41, Jacana – R. Volot – 51, NHPA S. Dalton 53, Aquila Photographics – T. Leach 54, Wildlife Studies Ltd 60, NHPA – A. Butler 67. Wildlife Studies Ltd 87. Cover: Newnes Books – Peter Loughran.

Index